Elements Of Life

Dr Manu Modi

India | USA | UK

Made with ❤ on the BookLeaf Publishing Platform
www.bookleafpub.in
www.bookleafpub.com

Dedication

This collection of poems is dedicated to everyone around us and to our Mother Earth, who has been endlessly generous, providing us with everything we need without asking for anything in return. It is our responsibility to give back to society and protect our natural resources so that we can leave behind a

healthier and more beautiful
planet for our future generations.

Preface

This collection of poems was an unexpected journey for us, as writing was never a part of our daily practice at the clinic. As a doctor, I have dedicated my life to my patients, and this experience of writing has given me the confidence to explore more avenues for sharing knowledge. Through this book, we hope to spread awareness and wisdom to a wider audience.

Acknowledgements

I extend my heartfelt gratitude to my dedicated team of doctors, whose support and encouragement helped bring this collection of poems to life. A special thanks to my family—my wife, Dr. Mona Modi, and my children, Dr. Manav Modi and Manya Modi—for their unwavering belief in me. I also express my deepest appreciation to my father, P.C. Modi, whose background in the judiciary and passion for Urdu writing have always been a source of inspiration.

My sincere thanks to BookLeaf Publications for making this journey possible. Lastly, my acknowledgments would be incomplete without a special mention of Dr. Kritika Sharma, a determined soul from a small town in Haryana, who persistently motivated me to take this step.

1. Who you are???

Some people will see you as strong
Some may consider you as weak

You will be considered as generous by some
Others will label you as miser

Some will consider you down to earth
Others may label you as arrogant

Some people may consider you the best
others may call you the worst.

The people around you will not agree and accept the way
you are

So only hear to your heart and that is who you are

2. Love

Love is a short word
Easy to spell and difficult to define

Love is overcoming obstacles
Facing challenges
Fighting together
Holding on and never letting it go

Love is realizing that
every hour
every minute
every second
was worth it because you did it all together

3. Rally

Crowds gather, hopes held high,
Promises shine, but soon they die.

Leaders speak with words so grand,
Yet nothing changes on this land.

Banners wave, the drums are loud,
False hopes given to the crowd.

Smiles fade when votes are cast,
Dreams are broken, like the past.

Again we wait, again we yearn,
But honesty may never return.

And the rally goes on and if this is democracy i dont
really need it!!

4. Watch

A watch upon the wrist so fine,
Tells time, both fleeting and divine.
Its ticking beats, a steady song,
Reminding us the days are long.

From dawn to dusk, it marks the hour,
Each second passing with its power.
A silent witness, it does not speak,
But in its face, the moments peek.

A timeless bond between us two,
The watch, the wearer, ever true.
In every tick, life moves along,
A fleeting journey, short yet strong.

5. AQI

The air feels heavy, hard to breathe,
A hidden danger we can't see.

The sky turns gray, the sun looks dim,
The air is filled with dust and grim.

It's hard to play, it's hard to run,
The air is bad for everyone.

Let's plant more trees and keep it clean,
So fresh, pure air can always be seen.

Together we can make it right,
For a future that's healthy and bright.

6. Friends

Friends are treasures, pure and true,
They stand by you in all you do.

Through laughs and tears, they're always near,
A source of joy, a listening ear.

They share your dreams, they lift your heart,
With friends, life's better from the start.

In every moment, dark or bright,
They bring you warmth, they bring you light.

Forever cherished, till the end,
Life is golden with a friend.

7. Money

Money shines, a tempting lure,
But it can't buy a heart that's pure.

It builds big homes, buys fancy things,
Yet can't give peace or joy it brings.

In gold and coins, some place their trust,
Forgetting kindness, love, and must.

It comes and goes, like waves at sea,
Not the key to what makes us free.

Use it wisely, let it not control,
For life's true wealth lies in the soul.

8. Doctors

In childhood, I've heard and seen,
A light so pure, so calm, serene.

And now I know, it must be true,
An angel walks this earth as you.

You're here to heal, to guide, to stay,
To chase the suffering far away.

With kindness bright and heart so free,
You bring the world true harmony.

The doctor is a comforting light
Guiding us through our darkest night

You are helpful and supportive in a way that warms our
heart
The thing that makes you special is a kind and generous
heart

You are brave during the darkest times as your existence
radiates light

Thankyou for the kindness and underdstanding you
gave
And hence the differnces made

9. Daughters

A daughter is a shining star,
Lighting paths both near and far.

With laughter sweet, she fills the air,
A heart so kind, beyond compare.

She brings the sun on cloudy days,
Her love shines bright in countless ways.

A gentle soul, yet strong and true,
Her dreams soar high, like skies so blue.

A treasure rare, a gift so dear,
A daughter's love will always cheer.

10. Smile

A smile can light the darkest days,
It sparks a joy in countless ways.

A curve so simple, yet so bright,
It turns the shadows into light.

It speaks a language, kind and true,
A gesture warm, for me and you.

A smile can heal a heart that's torn,
Or lift a soul that's bruised and worn.

In every smile, a story told,
A silent grace, a love to hold.

11. Companion

A companion stays through thick and thin,
A friend who helps you smile and win.

They walk beside you, hand in hand,
Through stormy skies or peaceful land.

They listen when your heart feels sore,
And cheer you up forevermore.

With laughter, kindness, love, and care,
A true companion is always there.

No matter where life takes you to,
A loyal friend will see you through.

12. Bharat

Bharat, our land so rich and wide,
Where rivers flow and mountains abide.

Fields of gold and forests green,
Beauty in every corner seen.

A land of culture, brave and free,
With wisdom deep as the endless sea.

Unity shines in every heart,
From every village to bustling mart.

Bharat, our pride, our sacred soil,
Forever we'll love you, with endless toil.

13. Time

Time moves fast, like a flowing stream,
Carrying us through every dream.

Minutes pass, they never stay,
Yesterday fades, it slips away.

Time can heal, but it can't wait,
It's always moving, never late.

A precious gift, we can't rewind,
Lost forever, once left behind.

So treasure now, make each day shine,
For time is yours, and it is mine.

14. Marriage

Marriage is a bond, both strong and true,
A journey of life for me and you.

Two hearts united, a promise made,
Through light and shadow, never to fade.

It's love and trust, and sometimes tears,
A partnership that grows with years.

It's laughter shared and burdens light,
A hand to hold through darkest night.

Together we stand, come joy or strife,
Marriage is the heart of a shared life.

15. Life and death

Life is a journey, a fleeting flame,
A path we walk, no two the same.

The sun will rise, the moon will set,
In time, all hearts must pay their debt.

Death's a door, not dark nor cold,
But a mystery, its truth untold.

Life blooms bright, then fades away,
Like the colors of a fleeting day.

Yet love and memories always remain,
In hearts that carry joy and pain.

16. My Dentist

My dentist's name is Dr. Modi.
He often says, Clean your teeth twice a day.
He often says, Rinse your mouth with warm water.
He often says, Eat one whole apple every day.

My dentist's name is Dr. Modi
He often says you will enjoy the treatment.
He often says I will make you love your dental journey.
He often says if you brush for 2 minutes, you will be able
to save your teeth for your life.

My dentist's name is Dr. Modi.
He often says if your mouth is healthy, your body will be
healthy.
He often says if you maintain your teeth, you will be
able to live longer.
He often says if your mouth smells fresh, you will have
lots of friends.

My dentist's name is Dr. Modi,
and he is my hero and a true inspiration.

17. Internet

The internet is a magic place,
Connecting people in every space.

With just one click, we learn and see,
A world of knowledge, wild and free.

Messages fly from near to far,
Videos stream like shooting stars.

But use it wisely, don't get lost,
Too much screen time has a cost.

A tool so grand, both fast and vast,
The internet makes the future last!

18. Road

Roads stretch far, both straight and wide,
Guiding us on every ride.

Through the hills and by the sea,
They take us where we wish to be.

Some are smooth, and some are rough,
Long and winding, tough and tough.

Lights and signs show us the way,
Helping drivers night and day.

With every turn, a tale unfolds,
As roads lead us to dreams untold.

19. Nature

Nature is bright, so fresh and free,
With tall green trees and buzzing bees.

The rivers flow, the flowers bloom,
The air is filled with sweet perfume.

The birds sing songs up in the sky,
As fluffy clouds go drifting by.

The sun shines bright, the breeze is cool,
The moonlight makes the night so full.

Nature's beauty is a gift so true,
Let's love and keep it fresh and new!

20. Water

Water flows in rivers wide,
Sparkling waves dance with the tide.

Raindrops fall from clouds so high,
Filling lakes as they pass by.

We drink, we wash, we swim, we play,
Water helps us every day.

Soft as mist and hard as ice,
A gift of nature, pure and nice.

Let's save each drop, both big and small,
For water is life—it's needed by all!

21. Goodbye

Goodbye is hard, but don't feel sad,
The time we shared makes my heart glad.

Though we must part and walk away,
Our memories bright will always stay.

A hug, a smile, one last goodbye,
But not forever—no need to cry.

New journeys wait, new paths to find,
Yet you'll remain in heart and mind.

So till we meet another day,
I send my love along your way!